Parenting Styles Authoritative

Balancing Love, Discipline, and Empowerment

Simi Subhramanian

Copyright © 2023 by Simi Subhramanian

Disclaimer: The information provided in this book is for general informational purposes only. The content is based on the topic of authoritative parenting styles and aims to provide insights into balancing love, discipline, and empowerment in parenting. Parenting is a deeply personal journey, and each child and family is unique. The concepts discussed in this book may not be applicable to every parenting situation. It is essential for parents to consider their child's individual needs, temperament, and developmental stage when applying parenting principles. The author and publisher disclaim any liability for any loss or damage incurred by the reader or any third party directly or indirectly as a result of the use or application of the information presented in this book. The content provided in this book should not be misconstrued as a replacement for professional advice or parenting guidance. Parenting is a complex endeavour, and the author encourages readers to seek additional resources and support from qualified professionals when facing parenting challenges or seeking personalized guidance.

Author Profile

Simi Subhramanian is an accomplished author and dedicated educator with a passion for teaching. She holds a range of qualifications in the teaching profession, including certifications from the Asian College of Teachers, TQUK (Training Qualifications UK), and Montessori Europe. With an extensive educational background, Simi brings a wealth of knowledge and expertise to her writing.

Simi's journey in education began at the Asian College of Teachers in Mumbai, India. There, she honed her teaching skills and gained a deep understanding of pedagogical principles. Armed with this foundation, she embarked on a mission to inspire and educate students of all ages through her writing.

Further enriching her qualifications, Simi pursued additional certifications from TQUK and Montessori Europe. These certifications expanded her repertoire of teaching methodologies and deepened her understanding of diverse learning styles. With these enhanced skills, she has been able to create engaging and effective educational content that caters to a wide range of learners.

Simi's writing reflects her commitment to excellence in education. She understands that effective teaching goes beyond imparting knowledge; it requires creativity, empathy, and the ability to connect with students on a deeper level. Her dedication to fostering a love of learning and promoting critical thinking is evident in her work.

Through her writing, Simi aims to inspire and empower students, encouraging them to reach their full potential. Her books and educational materials cover a wide range of subjects, from language arts to science and mathematics. Simi's approach emphasizes active learning, interactivity, and real-world applications to ensure students grasp concepts thoroughly.

With her diverse qualifications and years of experience in the teaching profession, Simi Subhramanian has established herself as a trusted and respected author in the education field. Her passion for teaching shines through in her writing, making her work both informative and engaging.

Simi continues to stay abreast of the latest developments in education and actively seeks innovative teaching approaches. By incorporating emerging trends and methodologies into her writing, she ensures that her educational materials remain relevant and effective.

Simi Subhramanian's author profile represents a seamless integration of her teaching qualifications from the Asian College of Teachers, TQUK, and Montessori Europe. Her expertise and dedication make her a valuable asset in the realm of educational literature, as she strives to make a positive impact on students' lives through her insightful and engaging content.

Introduction

In the intricate tapestry of parenthood, we all strive to be the guiding light for our children, shaping their destinies with love, discipline, and empowerment. Yet, the path to becoming a truly effective and nurturing parent is often shrouded in uncertainty, riddled with questions and doubts. How can we find the perfect balance between tenderness and firmness? How do we foster independence without losing the precious connection we share with our children? As we embark on this parenting journey, the authoritative style emerges as a beacon of hope, illuminating the way forward.

Welcome to "Parenting Styles Authoritative: Balancing Love, Discipline, and Empowerment." Within these pages, we invite you to explore the extraordinary world of authoritative parenting, where the power of love intertwines with the strength of discipline, and the nurturing embrace of empowerment leads to extraordinary growth.

Picture a parenting style that harmonizes the warmth of affectionate hugs with the wisdom of clear boundaries, where love becomes the bedrock upon which discipline stands tall, unwavering and just. This is the world of the authoritative parent - one who understands that true authority stems not from fear but from trust, not from control but from guidance, not from dominance but from respect.

In this book, we embark on a journey that will transform your perception of parenting. Drawing from the latest research, psychological insights, and real-life experiences, we unravel the essence of authoritative parenting, demystifying its core principles, and equipping you with the invaluable tools to apply them in your own unique family dynamic.

As you flip through the pages, you will discover that authoritative parenting is not a rigid set of rules but a dance of flexibility and adaptability. It is a melody that ebbs and flows, adjusting its tempo to the needs of each child, nurturing their individuality, and celebrating their strengths.

But this journey is not only about your children; it is also about you – the parent. We understand the challenges you face, the doubts that cloud your mind, and the emotional roller-coaster you ride. That's why we've woven threads of self-care, resilience, and emotional intelligence into the fabric of this book, helping you thrive as a parent and as an individual.

Get ready to explore the magic that happens when love intertwines with discipline, empowering your children to become the best versions of

themselves. Prepare to witness your relationship with your child blossom into a profound connection, built on mutual respect and trust. Are you ready to embark on this transformational journey, where you become the authoritative, loving, and empowered parent your child needs?

In "Parenting Styles Authoritative: Balancing Love, Discipline, and Empowerment," we invite you to open your heart, embrace the challenges, and embark on a quest to create a loving and nurturing haven for your family. Together, let us unlock the secrets of authoritative parenting and witness the beauty of its transformative power.

Chapter 1

Understanding the Authoritative Parenting Style

In the world of parenting, no style has garnered as much attention and acclaim as the authoritative approach. Unlike the traditional autocratic style that demands blind obedience or the permissive style that lacks structure, authoritative parenting strikes a delicate balance between love and discipline, fostering an environment of empowerment and growth. In this chapter, we will embark on a journey to deeply understand the authoritative parenting style, exploring its origins, fundamental principles, and the extensive research that supports its efficacy.

The Roots of Authoritative Parenting

The concept of authoritative parenting finds its roots in the work of psychologist Diana Baumrind in the 1960s. Through her extensive research, Baumrind identified three primary parenting styles – authoritarian, permissive, and authoritative. Her pioneering studies shed light on the profound impact of parenting approaches on child development and behaviour.

The Key Characteristics of Authoritative Parenting

Authoritative parenting is characterized by a unique blend of love, warmth, and firmness. It is neither overly restrictive nor lax in setting boundaries. Instead, it promotes a balanced approach that nurtures emotional well-being while instilling a sense of responsibility and accountability.

Love and Emotional Connection

At the heart of authoritative parenting lies genuine love and emotional connection between parent and child. Warmth, affection, and support form the foundation of this style. Children raised in such an environment feel secure, valued, and confident in expressing their emotions.

Clear and Consistent Boundaries

While authoritative parents are loving and emotionally available, they also understand the importance of setting clear and consistent boundaries. These boundaries provide children with a sense of structure and predictability, allowing them to understand expectations and consequences.

Open Communication

Healthy communication is an essential element of the authoritative parenting style. Parents who adopt this approach actively listen to their children, empathize with their concerns, and encourage open dialogue. This fosters trust and mutual understanding between parent and child.

Responsiveness and Support

Authoritative parents are attuned to their child's needs and provide appropriate support and guidance. They are responsive to their child's emotions, seeking to understand their perspective and offering comfort during challenging times.

Encouragement of Independence

One hallmark of authoritative parenting is the promotion of independence and autonomy in children. Parents in this style allow their children to make age-appropriate decisions, learn from their mistakes, and develop a sense of self-reliance.

The Impact of Authoritative Parenting on Child Development

The influence of authoritative parenting on child development has been extensively studied and validated by researchers worldwide. Numerous studies have shown that children raised with authoritative parenting tend to exhibit a range of positive outcomes, both during childhood and into adulthood.

Emotional Intelligence and Social Competence

Children raised in an authoritative environment tend to develop higher emotional intelligence and social competence. The loving and responsive nature of authoritative parenting fosters empathy and an understanding of emotions, enabling children to navigate social interactions with ease.

Academic Achievement

Authoritative parenting has been linked to higher academic achievement in children. The balanced approach of setting expectations while providing support and encouragement creates an environment conducive to learning and intellectual growth.

Self-Esteem and Confidence

Children raised with authoritative parenting are more likely to develop healthy self-esteem and self-confidence. The combination of love and discipline helps them recognize their strengths, overcome challenges, and build a positive self-image.

Emotional Resilience

The supportive and empowering nature of authoritative parenting contributes to the development of emotional resilience in children. They learn to cope with adversity, bounce back from setbacks, and view challenges as opportunities for growth.

The Intersection of Culture and Authoritative Parenting

It is essential to recognize that parenting styles are influenced by cultural norms, beliefs, and values. While authoritative parenting is widely celebrated for its positive outcomes, its implementation may vary across different cultures. Understanding the cultural context helps parents tailor authoritative parenting to meet the needs and expectations of their unique family dynamics.

Challenges and Potential Pitfalls

Despite its numerous benefits, authoritative parenting is not without its challenges. Parents may sometimes struggle to strike the right balance between being nurturing and maintaining discipline. It requires constant self-awareness, adaptability, and patience to grow into an authoritative parent effectively.

Avoiding Authoritarian Tendencies

There is a fine line between authoritative and authoritarian parenting styles. Authoritative parents must be cautious not to slip into overly controlling behaviours that might undermine the positive effects of this approach.

Handling Resistance and Rebellion

As children grow older, they may challenge the boundaries set by their authoritative parents. Understanding how to navigate through teenage rebellion while maintaining a healthy parent-child relationship is a crucial aspect of this

parenting style.

Embracing the Journey of Authoritative Parenting

Parenting, in any style, is a journey filled with growth, learning, and love. Embracing the authoritative parenting style requires dedication, understanding, and a willingness to evolve alongside your child. In the subsequent chapters, we will delve deeper into practical strategies and techniques that will empower you to become an authoritative parent - one who balances love, discipline, and empowerment to create a nurturing and thriving family environment. So, let us embark on this transformative journey together and witness the extraordinary impact of authoritative parenting on our children's lives.

Chapter 2
Love: The Bedrock of Authority

Love is the heartbeat of parenthood, the source from which all other elements of authoritative parenting flow. In this chapter, we delve into the profound significance of love in the authoritative parenting style. We explore the transformative power of affectionate connections between parent and child, the impact of secure emotional bonds on child development, and the ways in which love forms the bedrock upon which authority stands tall.

The Essence of Love in Parenting

Love is not merely an emotion; it is an action, a commitment, and a way of being. In authoritative parenting, love serves as the guiding force that shapes the parent-child relationship. It is the emotional currency that fosters trust, respect, and a deep sense of belonging.

Unconditional Love

At the core of authoritative parenting is unconditional love. It is a love that transcends mistakes, failures, and imperfections. When children feel loved unconditionally, they develop a sense of security and assurance, knowing that their parents will support and cherish them, regardless of the circumstances.

Love as a Source of Comfort

Love acts as a soothing balm during times of distress and uncertainty. In moments of sadness or anxiety, a parent's loving presence can provide a safe harbor for children to find solace and reassurance.

The Impact of Love on Child Development

Numerous studies have highlighted the profound impact of love and affection on child development. The emotional connections formed during childhood lay the foundation for a child's emotional intelligence, social competence, and overall well-being.

Building Secure Attachment

Secure attachment between parent and child is a cornerstone of emotional development. A securely attached child feels confident exploring the world, knowing they have a nurturing and responsive caregiver to return to when needed.

Emotional Regulation and Resilience

Children who experience love and emotional support tend to develop better emotional regulation and resilience. Love provides a buffer against stress and adversity, enabling children to cope with challenges more effectively.

Healthy Self-Esteem

Love and positive reinforcement contribute to the development of a healthy sense of self-worth. When children feel loved and accepted for who they are, they are more likely to develop positive self-esteem and confidence.

Empathy and Compassion

Love nurtures empathy and compassion in children. As they experience loving and caring relationships, they learn to understand and empathize with the emotions of others, fostering healthy social connections.

Expressing Love in Authoritative Parenting

Love is not limited to words but is demonstrated through actions and behaviours. In authoritative parenting, expressing love is an ongoing process that creates a nurturing and affirming environment for children to thrive.

Physical Affection

Physical affection, such as hugging, cuddling, and holding hands, is a powerful way to convey love and care to children. These gestures create a sense of safety and warmth, promoting emotional closeness.

Active Listening and Presence

Listening attentively to a child's thoughts, feelings, and concerns communicates love and respect. Being fully present during interactions demonstrates that a child's voice is heard and valued.

Praise and Encouragement

Encouraging words and genuine praise uplift a child's spirit and reinforce positive behaviour. Acknowledging a child's efforts and achievements fosters a

sense of accomplishment and motivation to continue striving.

Quality Time

Spending quality time with children strengthens the parent-child bond. Engaging in shared activities and creating lasting memories contribute to a sense of connectedness and belonging.

Love as the Foundation for Effective Discipline

Discipline, when rooted in love, becomes a powerful tool for guiding children towards positive behaviour and growth. In authoritative parenting, discipline is not about punishment but about teaching and understanding.

Setting Clear Expectations

Love and discipline go hand in hand when parents set clear expectations for behaviour and communicate them with love and empathy. Children understand what is expected of them and why certain boundaries are in place.

Consequences with Compassion

When a child's behaviour requires consequences, applying them with compassion and understanding is crucial. Instead of inducing fear, consequences become opportunities for learning and personal growth.

Teaching Emotional Regulation

Love empowers parents to teach children how to regulate their emotions effectively. Instead of suppressing emotions, children are encouraged to express and understand them constructively.

Consistency and Predictability

Consistency in applying rules and consequences provides a sense of stability and predictability for children. They understand that certain behaviours lead to specific outcomes, promoting a sense of fairness and trust.

Cultivating a Loving Parenting Mindset

Embracing a loving parenting mindset is a continuous journey of self-awareness and growth. It involves recognizing and addressing one's own emotional triggers and biases to create a nurturing and loving environment for children.

Embracing Vulnerability

Loving parenting requires vulnerability – the willingness to be open, empathetic, and emotionally available for our children. It involves acknowledging our own imperfections and modelling healthy emotional expression.

Practising Self-Compassion

Parenting with love means extending the same compassion we offer our children to ourselves. Being kind to ourselves during challenging times allows us to be more patient and understanding parents.

Seeking Support and Connection

Building a supportive network of friends, family, or parenting groups can provide valuable encouragement and understanding. Sharing experiences and seeking advice from others helps in navigating the parenting journey with love and resilience.

The Love-Fueled Authority

In the realm of authoritative parenting, love and authority are not opposing forces but complementary energies. Love fuels the authority wielded by parents, making it a force of guidance, growth, and empowerment.

Trust and Respect

Children raised with love-infused authority develop a deep trust and respect for their parents. They understand that parental guidance comes from a place of care and concern for their well-being.

Instilling Internal Discipline

Authoritative parents nurture internal discipline in their children, empowering them to make responsible choices guided by their own values and moral compass.

Independence and Decision-Making

As children grow, the love-fueled authority encourages independence and autonomy. They learn to make decisions with confidence, knowing that their parents provide a supportive and guiding presence.

Love in Action: Stories of Impact

Real-life stories of families practising authoritative parenting illustrate the profound impact of love on children's lives. These narratives exemplify the transformative power of a loving parent-child relationship.

The Eternal Legacy of Love

The love we instil in our children leaves an indelible mark on their lives, shaping their character, choices, and relationships. As we embrace the authoritative parenting style, let us remember that love is the eternal legacy we gift to our children, fostering a bright and compassionate future for generations to come.

As we continue on this journey, let love be the compass that guides us, and authority the anchor that keeps us steady in nurturing and raising happy, confident, and compassionate individuals.

Chapter 3
Discipline: Nurturing Responsibility and Accountability

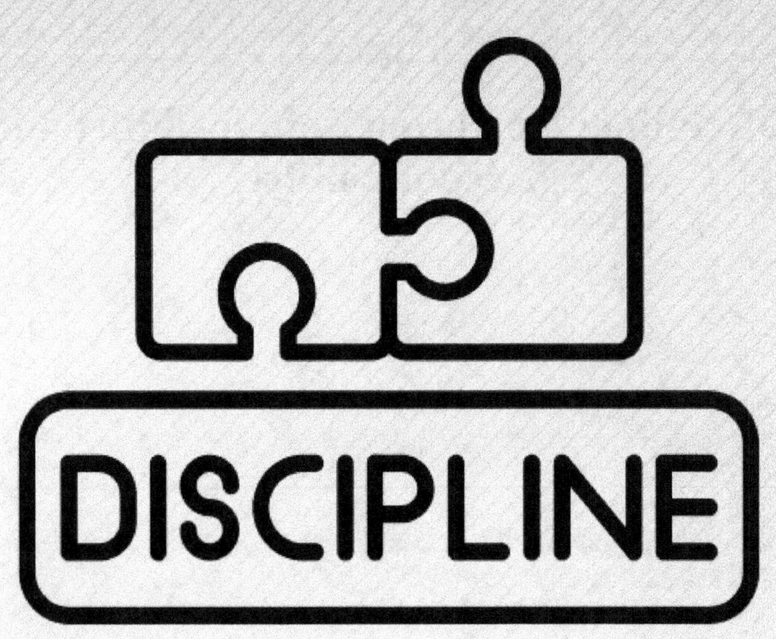
DISCIPLINE

In the realm of authoritative parenting, discipline is not about punishment or control; it is a transformative tool for nurturing responsibility and accountability in children. In this chapter, we delve into the profound importance of discipline within the authoritative parenting style. We explore the principles and techniques that promote positive behaviour, self-regulation, and a deep understanding of consequences, all while fostering a loving and respectful parent-child relationship.

Redefining Discipline in Authoritative Parenting

Discipline, in the context of authoritative parenting, is a positive and constructive approach to teaching children about boundaries, values, and responsible decision-making. Rather than imposing strict rules, this style of discipline seeks to guide children towards making informed choices and understanding the consequences of their actions.

Discipline as Teaching

At its core, discipline is a form of teaching. It involves helping children develop self-control, emotional regulation, and problem-solving skills. Through discipline, parents have the opportunity to mold their children's character, equipping them with essential life skills.

Balancing Structure and Flexibility

Authoritative parents strike a balance between providing a structured environment and being flexible enough to adapt to their child's individual needs and developmental stage. This approach fosters a sense of security and empowerment in children.

Fostering Independence

Discipline in authoritative parenting is not about controlling every aspect of a child's life. Instead, it encourages children to take ownership of their actions, empowering them to make responsible choices independently.

The Role of Clear Expectations

Clear and consistent expectations are a vital aspect of authoritative discipline. Children need to understand what is expected of them to navigate their world

confidently and make informed decisions.

Age-Appropriate Expectations

Setting age-appropriate expectations ensures that children can meet the challenges presented to them, fostering a sense of competence and accomplishment.

Communicating Expectations with Love

Authoritative parents communicate expectations with love and empathy. They provide context and reasoning behind rules, helping children understand the importance of following guidelines.

Establishing Family Rules Together

Involving children in the process of establishing family rules promotes a sense of ownership and cooperation. When children contribute to rule-making, they are more likely to follow them willingly.

Positive Discipline Techniques

Positive discipline techniques form the cornerstone of authoritative parenting. These strategies focus on guiding children toward positive behaviour and learning opportunities.

Natural Consequences

Natural consequences allow children to experience the direct outcome of their actions, helping them understand cause and effect. This approach teaches responsibility and accountability.

Logical Consequences

Logical consequences are related to the misbehaviour and are designed to be reasonable and instructive. Unlike punishments, logical consequences are intended to teach and guide children towards better choices.

Time-In, Not Time-Out

Instead of using punitive time-outs, authoritative parents employ "time-in" as a way to connect with their child during challenging moments. Time-in allows parents to address the underlying emotions and coach the child towards better behaviour.

Reinforcing Positive Behaviour

Recognizing and praising positive behaviour reinforces the desired actions and encourages children to continue making responsible choices.

Addressing Challenging Behaviour with Empathy

Children may display challenging behaviour due to a variety of reasons, such as frustration, stress, or lack of emotional regulation. Empathy and understanding are crucial when addressing these behaviours.

Identifying Triggers and Emotions

Authoritative parents seek to identify the underlying triggers and emotions that lead to challenging behaviour. By understanding the root causes, they can address the behaviour more effectively.

Emotional Coaching

Emotional coaching involves acknowledging and validating a child's emotions, teaching them how to express feelings constructively, and finding appropriate solutions to address the emotional needs.

Calm Parenting in the Face of Disobedience

Remaining calm during moments of disobedience is essential in authoritative parenting. A composed parent models emotional regulation and demonstrates how to handle challenging situations with grace and patience.

Consistency and Predictability

Consistency in disciplinary approaches is crucial for children to understand and internalize family rules and values. Predictability helps children feel secure, knowing what to expect in various situations.

Unified Parenting Approach

In authoritative parenting, both parents ideally adopt a unified approach to discipline. Presenting a united front helps children understand that family rules are shared values and expectations.

Family Meetings

Family meetings provide an opportunity to discuss and address disciplinary matters collectively. These meetings encourage open communication, problem-solving, and collaboration among family members.

Shaping Character and Responsibility

Authoritative discipline is not just about correcting behaviour, it is about instilling character and fostering a sense of responsibility in children.

Accountability for Actions

Encouraging children to take responsibility for their actions helps them understand the impact of their choices on themselves and others. This sense of accountability cultivates integrity and self-awareness.

Learning from Mistakes

Authoritative parents view mistakes as opportunities for growth and learning. By helping children analyse their actions and consequences, parents foster resilience and a growth mindset.

Encouraging Problem-Solving

When faced with challenges, children in authoritative households are encouraged to engage in problem-solving. This empowers them to find creative solutions and take ownership of their decisions.

Discipline and Love: A Harmonious Union

In authoritative parenting, discipline and love are intertwined, forming a harmonious union. Love underpins the discipline, making it a constructive and nurturing process.

Correcting Behaviour with Empathy

When disciplining, authoritative parents correct behaviour with empathy, understanding that their child's actions are not indicative of their worth as individuals.

Reinforcing Love during Discipline

During moments of discipline, parents reaffirm their love for their children. This ensures that children do not equate discipline with a lack of love or acceptance.

Building Trust through Discipline

Authoritative discipline builds a foundation of trust between parent and child. Trust allows children to feel safe in seeking guidance and support from their parents.

Trusting in the Child's Abilities

Authoritative parents demonstrate trust in their child's capabilities by allowing them to make age-appropriate decisions and learn from their experiences.

Honouring Parental Promises

Fulfilling promises made to children demonstrates reliability and trustworthiness. Children learn to trust their parents' words and intentions.

Discipline in Difficult Circumstances

In challenging circumstances, such as divorce or relocation, maintaining authoritative discipline is essential for providing stability and support to children.

Consistency in Times of Change

During transitional periods, remaining consistent in discipline provides children with a sense of stability and predictability.

Empowering Communication

Open and honest communication during difficult times helps children process their emotions and feel supported.

The Ongoing Journey of Discipline

Discipline in authoritative parenting is an ongoing journey, adapting and evolving as children grow and develop. Parenting with love and authority requires patience, flexibility, and a commitment to continuous learning.

Reflecting and Adjusting

Authoritative parents reflect on their disciplinary approaches, assessing what works best for each child, and adjusting strategies as needed.

Embracing Mistakes and Learning Opportunities

Parenting is not perfect, and mistakes will happen. Authoritative parents embrace these moments as learning opportunities for both themselves and their children.

Celebrating Progress

Celebrating the progress made by children in their behaviour and decision-making reinforces positive growth and motivates further improvement.

Chapter 4
Empowerment: Cultivating Confidence and Independence

Empowerment is the cornerstone of authoritative parenting, unlocking the potential for children to become confident, independent, and resilient individuals. In this chapter, we delve into the transformative power of empowerment within the authoritative parenting style. We explore how parents can foster a sense of self-worth, autonomy, and a growth mindset in their children, laying the foundation for a successful and fulfilling future.

The Essence of Empowerment in Parenting

Empowerment is the process of enabling and supporting children to take charge of their lives, make informed decisions, and develop a sense of agency. In authoritative parenting, empowerment is not about control or dominance, it is about nurturing self-assurance and confidence.

Encouraging Self-Expression

Authoritative parents encourage their children to express their thoughts, feelings, and opinions freely. By valuing their input, children develop a sense of self-worth and confidence in their ideas.

Supporting Individuality

Empowerment embraces the uniqueness of each child. Authoritative parents celebrate their children's individual strengths and interests, allowing them to explore their passions and talents.

Fostering a Growth Mindset

Authoritative parents promote a growth mindset, emphasizing the belief that abilities and intelligence can be developed through effort and perseverance. This mindset encourages children to embrace challenges and view failures as opportunities to learn and grow.

Building Resilience

Empowerment instils resilience in children, enabling them to bounce back from setbacks and adversity. They learn to view challenges as stepping stones toward achieving their goals.

Autonomy and Decision-Making

Empowerment in authoritative parenting involves granting children appropriate autonomy and the opportunity to make decisions that impact their lives.

Age-Appropriate Autonomy

Authoritative parents provide children with age-appropriate autonomy, allowing them to take on responsibilities that match their developmental stage.

Guided Decision-Making

Empowerment does not mean leaving children to make critical decisions on their own. Authoritative parents offer guidance and support during the decision-making process.

Learning from Choices

When children make decisions, they learn from both successful and unsuccessful outcomes. These experiences build confidence in their ability to make informed choices.

Encouraging Responsibility and Accountability

Empowerment and responsibility go hand in hand. In authoritative parenting, children are encouraged to take responsibility for their actions and understand the consequences of their decisions.

Age-Appropriate Responsibilities

Authoritative parents assign age-appropriate responsibilities that allow children to contribute to the family and learn the value of accountability.

Understanding Consequences

Children in authoritative households are guided to understand the consequences of their actions, fostering a sense of accountability for their behaviour.

Supporting Goal Setting and Achievement

Empowerment involves helping children set and achieve meaningful goals, cultivating a sense of accomplishment and motivation.

Identifying Personal Goals

Authoritative parents encourage children to identify their own goals, whether academic, extracurricular, or personal, and provide support in working towards them.

Celebrating Achievements

Celebrating achievements, big and small, reinforces children's belief in their abilities and encourages them to aim higher.

Nurturing Independence

Empowerment in authoritative parenting nurtures independence in children, allowing them to gradually become self-reliant.

Encouraging Self-Help Skills

Authoritative parents encourage children to develop self-help skills, such as dressing themselves, tying shoelaces, or preparing simple meals.

Promoting Problem-Solving

Empowered children are confident in their ability to solve problems. Authoritative parents offer guidance but also allow children the space to think critically and find solutions on their own.

Allowing Room for Mistakes

Independence involves making mistakes and learning from them. Authoritative parents create an environment where children feel safe to learn from their errors without fear of judgment.

Encouraging Extracurricular Exploration

Empowerment embraces the opportunity for children to explore a range of extracurricular activities that align with their interests and passions.

Supporting Passions

Authoritative parents support their children's interests, whether it be sports, arts, music, or any other pursuit that brings them joy.

Balancing Commitments

While encouraging exploration, authoritative parents help children strike a balance between their various interests and commitments.

Building Self-Confidence and Self-Esteem

Empowerment in authoritative parenting helps children develop a strong sense of self-confidence and healthy self-esteem.

Positive Affirmations

Authoritative parents offer positive affirmations and validation to reinforce their children's sense of self-worth.

Recognizing Effort

Acknowledging a child's effort, even if the outcome is not perfect, fosters a growth mindset and a belief in their abilities.

Encouraging Self-Reflection

Empowered children engage in self-reflection, celebrating their successes and identifying areas for improvement.

Respecting Boundaries and Choices

Empowerment respects children's boundaries and choices, encouraging open communication and mutual understanding.

Respecting Privacy

Authoritative parents respect their children's need for privacy and personal space, fostering a trusting and secure relationship.

Active Listening

Empowerment involves active listening and empathetic understanding of a child's thoughts and feelings.

The Role of Effective Communication

Effective communication is fundamental in empowering children. It strengthens the parent-child bond and allows for open and honest expression.

Active Listening

Authoritative parents practice active listening, giving full attention to their child's words and feelings.

Empathetic Understanding

Empowerment involves empathetic understanding, validating a child's emotions and experiences.

Encouraging Open Dialogue

Creating a culture of open dialogue allows children to share their thoughts and concerns without fear of judgment.

Empowerment through Role Modelling

Authoritative parents model the qualities of empowerment they seek to instil in their children.

Modelling Confidence and Resilience

Demonstrating confidence in one's abilities and resilience in the face of challenges sets an example for children to follow.

Embracing Lifelong Learning

Authoritative parents embrace lifelong learning and growth, showing their children the value of continuous improvement.

Seeking Balance and Self-Care

Modelling a balanced approach to life and prioritizing self-care teaches children the importance of nurturing their own well-being.

Empowerment in Difficult Times

Empowerment is especially crucial during difficult times, such as transitions or challenging life events.

Providing Support and Assurance

Authoritative parents offer emotional support and assurance during difficult times, allowing children to navigate through challenges with confidence.

Encouraging Problem-Solving and Coping

Empowerment equips children with problem-solving skills and coping mechanisms to handle challenging situations effectively.

The Ongoing Journey of Empowerment

Empowerment is a continuous journey that evolves with children as they grow and develop. It requires dedication, patience, and an unwavering commitment to supporting the growth and potential of each child.

Celebrating Progress and Growth

Acknowledging and celebrating the progress made by children reinforces their belief in their abilities and encourages further growth.

Embracing the Uniqueness of Each Child

Empowerment respects and embraces the uniqueness of each child, recognizing that every child's journey is different.

Nurturing a Culture of Empowerment

Creating a culture of empowerment in the family fosters an environment where children feel supported and valued.

As we continue on this transformative journey of authoritative parenting, let us remember that empowerment is the key that unlocks the full potential of our children. By nurturing their confidence, independence, and resilience, we lay the foundation for them to become thriving and fulfilled individuals. Together, let us embark on this empowering path, guiding our children to embrace their true selves and embark on a journey of self-discovery and success.

Chapter 5

Communication: The Bridge between Parent and Child

Communication forms the vital bridge connecting parents and children in the journey of authoritative parenting. In this chapter, we explore the profound significance of effective communication within the authoritative parenting style. We delve into the principles and strategies that promote open dialogue, understanding, and mutual respect, fostering a deep and meaningful parent-child connection.

The Power of Effective Communication

Effective communication is the cornerstone of a strong and nurturing parent-child relationship. It is the conduit through which thoughts, emotions, and ideas are exchanged, creating a deep understanding and bond between parents and children.

Building Trust and Connection

Open and honest communication builds trust and connection between parents and children. When children feel heard and understood, they are more likely to share their thoughts and concerns.

Fostering Emotional Intelligence

Communication enables children to express and understand their emotions, fostering emotional intelligence and self-awareness.

Strengthening Parent-Child Attachment

A strong parent-child attachment is nurtured through positive and responsive communication. This attachment becomes the foundation for a child's healthy emotional development.

Resolving Conflicts Peacefully

Effective communication helps parents and children navigate conflicts peacefully and find constructive solutions.

Active Listening: The Heart of Effective Communication

Active listening is a fundamental aspect of effective communication in authoritative parenting. It involves being fully present and attentive when listening to a child's thoughts and feelings.

Giving Undivided Attention

When engaging in conversations, authoritative parents give their children undivided attention, demonstrating that their words are valued.

Listening Without Judgment

Active listening involves suspending judgment and allowing children to express themselves without fear of criticism.

Validating Emotions

Authoritative parents validate their child's emotions, showing understanding and empathy for their feelings.

Reflecting and Clarifying

Repeating and clarifying what the child has shared ensures that parents understand their child's perspective accurately.

Encouraging Open Dialogue

In authoritative parenting, open dialogue encourages children to share their thoughts, concerns, and ideas freely.

Creating a Safe Space

Authoritative parents create a safe and non-judgmental space where children feel comfortable sharing their thoughts.

Welcoming Different Perspectives

Encouraging open dialogue means respecting different perspectives and opinions, even if they differ from the parent's own.

Being Approachable

Authoritative parents are approachable and receptive, making it easy for

children to initiate conversations.

Prompting Conversations

Asking open-ended questions and initiating discussions on various topics prompt meaningful conversations.

Nurturing Emotional Expression

Emotionally healthy children are encouraged to express their feelings, thoughts, and concerns without hesitation.

Verbal and Non-Verbal Expression

Authoritative parents encourage both verbal and non-verbal forms of emotional expression, allowing children to communicate in ways that feel most comfortable to them.

Labelling and Validating Emotions

Helping children identify and label their emotions validates their experiences and encourages emotional expression.

Modelling Healthy Expression

Parents model healthy emotional expression by expressing their own feelings in a constructive and respectful manner.

Using Art and Play for Expression

Younger children may find it easier to express themselves through art, play, or other creative activities. Authoritative parents provide opportunities for these forms of expression.

The Art of Constructive Feedback

Constructive feedback is a crucial element of communication in authoritative parenting. It helps children understand areas of improvement while reinforcing positive behaviour.

Specific and Positive Feedback

Authoritative parents offer specific and positive feedback, highlighting a child's efforts and achievements.

Encouraging a Growth Mindset

Constructive feedback encourages a growth mindset by focusing on learning and improvement rather than on failure.

Balancing Praise and Critique

Balancing praise with areas for improvement ensures that children receive a well-rounded perspective on their actions.

Timing and Delivery

Offering feedback at appropriate times and using a supportive tone is essential in authoritative communication.

Managing Conflicts with Respect

Conflict is a natural part of human interactions. Authoritative parents manage conflicts with respect and understanding.

Staying Calm and Composed

During conflicts, authoritative parents model emotional regulation by staying calm and composed.

Active Problem-Solving

Engaging in active problem-solving during conflicts helps children understand how to address challenges constructively.

Finding Common Ground

Seeking common ground and compromising during conflicts fosters mutual understanding and resolution.

Offering Apologies and Forgiveness

When necessary, parents and children practice offering apologies and forgiveness, demonstrating the importance of repairing relationships after conflicts.

Encouraging Communication during Challenging Times

Open communication is especially important during challenging times, such as adolescence or family transitions.

Supporting Adolescents' Communication

Encouraging open communication during adolescence helps children navigate the complexities of this developmental stage.

Emotional Support during Transitions

During family transitions or challenging times, authoritative parents offer emotional support and encourage children to express their feelings.

Embracing Technology in Communication

In the digital age, technology can be a valuable tool for communication in authoritative parenting.

Setting Boundaries for Technology Use

Authoritative parents establish boundaries for technology use, ensuring that it does not interfere with family communication.

Using Technology for Positive Communication

Technology can be utilized for positive communication, such as sharing updates or engaging in virtual family activities.

Balancing In-Person and Virtual Communication

While technology facilitates communication, authoritative parents maintain a balance by prioritizing in-person interactions.

Empathy and Understanding in Communication

Empathy is a core aspect of effective communication in authoritative parenting.

Putting Yourself in Their Shoes

Empathizing with children involves trying to understand their perspective and experiences.

Acknowledging Emotions

Acknowledging a child's emotions demonstrates empathy and validates their feelings.

Responding with Compassion

Responding with compassion during difficult conversations fosters trust and emotional connection.

Building a Culture of Communication

Creating a culture of communication is an ongoing process that involves consistent effort and commitment.

Making Time for Communication

Authoritative parents prioritize communication by setting aside dedicated time for family conversations.

Establishing Family Rituals

Family rituals, such as meals or outings, provide opportunities for regular communication and bonding.

Encouraging Sibling Communication

Empowerment extends to sibling relationships, with authoritative parents fostering open communication among siblings.

Empowering Children's Voices

Empowerment in communication involves valuing and respecting children's perspectives and ideas.

Involving Children in Decision-Making

Authoritative parents involve children in family decisions, fostering a sense of ownership and contribution.

Encouraging Advocacy

Empowered children are encouraged to advocate for their needs and express their preferences.

Supporting Initiatives and Creativity

Supporting children's initiatives and creative ideas fosters their self-confidence and sense of agency.

Multicultural Communication in the Global Age

In an increasingly global and multicultural world, authoritative parents embrace the value of effective cross-cultural communication.

Embracing Diversity

Authoritative parents teach their children to embrace diversity and respect different cultural perspectives.

Learning from Cross-Cultural Interactions

Cross-cultural interactions present learning opportunities for children to broaden their understanding of the world.

Cultivating Cultural Sensitivity

Cultivating cultural sensitivity and open-mindedness fosters respectful and meaningful communication in diverse settings.

The Journey of Lifelong Communication

Effective communication is a lifelong journey in authoritative parenting, evolving and adapting as children grow and circumstances change.

Continued Learning and Growth

Authoritative parents continue to learn and grow as communicators, adapting their approach to meet the changing needs of their children.

Maintaining a Strong Parent-Child Connection

Through effective communication, authoritative parents maintain a strong and enduring connection with their children, even as they enter adulthood.

Embracing the Unpredictable

Communication in authoritative parenting embraces the unpredictability of life, facing challenges with resilience and openness.

As we continue on this journey of authoritative parenting, let us remember that communication is the lifeline that strengthens our bond with our children. By fostering open dialogue, empathy, and understanding, we build a bridge that connects us, empowering our children to navigate through life with confidence, resilience, and a deep sense of belonging. Together, let us embrace the power of effective communication and create a nurturing and loving environment that allows our children to thrive and fulfil their potential.

Chapter 6
Handling Challenges and Conflict

Challenges and conflicts are an inevitable part of parenting, and in the context of authoritative parenting, they present valuable opportunities for growth and learning. In this chapter, we explore the art of handling challenges and conflicts with compassion, empathy, and effective strategies. We delve into the principles and techniques that enable parents to navigate through difficult situations, strengthen the parent-child relationship, and promote positive resolutions.

Embracing Challenges as Opportunities

In authoritative parenting, challenges are not seen as obstacles but as opportunities for growth and development. Embracing challenges with a positive mindset allows parents to approach them with resilience and creativity.

Fostering a Growth Mindset

Authoritative parents encourage a growth mindset, where challenges are viewed as stepping stones toward progress and learning.

Learning from Adversity

Challenges provide valuable lessons for both parents and children, offering insights into problem-solving and emotional resilience.

Modelling Positive Coping Mechanisms

Parents model positive coping mechanisms during challenging times, teaching children how to handle stress and adversity constructively.

Effective Strategies for Conflict Resolution

Conflict is a natural part of human interactions, and in authoritative parenting, it is addressed with a focus on understanding, empathy, and cooperation.

Active Listening during Conflicts

Listening attentively to a child's perspective during conflicts fosters understanding and validates their feelings.

Maintaining Emotional Regulation

Authoritative parents maintain emotional regulation during conflicts, ensuring that discussions remain constructive and respectful.

Finding Common Ground

Seeking common ground and areas of agreement during conflicts facilitates positive resolution.

Encouraging Win-Win Solutions

Authoritative parents promote win-win solutions, where both parties feel satisfied with the outcome of the conflict.

Nurturing Emotional Intelligence during Challenges

Challenges provide opportunities for children to develop emotional intelligence, and authoritative parents play a crucial role in nurturing this aspect.

Validating Emotions

Acknowledging and validating children's emotions during challenges helps them process their feelings effectively.

Encouraging Emotional Expression

Authoritative parents encourage children to express their emotions in healthy and constructive ways.

Teaching Coping Strategies

Equipping children with coping strategies during challenging times empowers them to navigate through difficulties with resilience.

Promoting Empathy and Understanding

Encouraging empathy and understanding toward others' perspectives builds emotional intelligence and strengthens relationships.

Addressing Behavioural Challenges with Love and Discipline

Behavioural challenges are common in parenting, and in authoritative parenting, they are addressed with a balanced approach of love and discipline.

Understanding the Root Causes

Authoritative parents seek to understand the underlying reasons behind behavioural challenges, addressing the root causes rather than just the surface behaviours.

Applying Positive Discipline Techniques

Positive discipline techniques, such as natural consequences and logical consequences, help guide children toward better behaviour.

Reinforcing Positive Behaviour

Reinforcing positive behaviour with praise and encouragement motivates children to continue making responsible choices.

Teaching Emotional Regulation

Emotional regulation is essential in addressing behavioural challenges, and authoritative parents teach children how to manage their emotions effectively.

Cultivating Resilience in the Face of Adversity

Resilience is a valuable trait that helps children bounce back from setbacks and challenges. Authoritative parents cultivate resilience through love, support, and encouragement.

Encouraging a "Can-Do" Attitude

Authoritative parents instil a "can-do" attitude in their children, promoting a sense of confidence in their abilities.

Embracing Mistakes as Learning Opportunities

Mistakes are viewed as learning opportunities in authoritative parenting,

fostering a growth mindset.

Providing Emotional Support

During challenging times, authoritative parents offer emotional support, helping children cope with stress and difficulties.

Modelling Resilience

Parents model resilience by handling their own challenges with determination and a positive outlook.

Empowering Children to Problem-Solve

Empowerment plays a vital role in helping children develop problem-solving skills during challenges.

Guiding the Problem-Solving Process

Authoritative parents provide guidance and support as children navigate through problem-solving.

Encouraging Critical Thinking

Encouraging critical thinking empowers children to analyse situations and make informed decisions.

Promoting Collaboration

Collaborative problem-solving fosters teamwork and effective communication between parents and children.

Handling Parenting Disagreements with Respect

In co-parenting situations, disagreements may arise, and handling them with respect and understanding is essential in authoritative parenting.

Active Communication

Active communication between co-parents promotes a unified approach in

addressing challenges.

Seeking Compromise

Seeking compromise and finding common ground ensures a harmonious co-parenting dynamic.

Focusing on the Child's Best Interests

Authoritative co-parents prioritize the child's best interests, putting their needs above personal disagreements.

Utilizing Mediation if Needed

Mediation can be beneficial in resolving co-parenting disagreements and fostering effective communication.

Cultivating a Supportive Environment during Life Transitions

Life transitions, such as moving, divorce, or the arrival of a new sibling, can be challenging for children. Authoritative parents create a supportive environment to help children navigate through these changes.

Communicating with Sensitivity

Communicating life transitions with sensitivity helps children process their emotions and adapt to the changes.

Providing Stability and Predictability

During transitions, providing stability and predictability in daily routines helps children feel secure.

Encouraging Expression of Feelings

Authoritative parents encourage children to express their feelings about the transitions, validating their emotions.

Offering Emotional Support and Reassurance

During life transitions, authoritative parents offer emotional support and reassurance, helping children adjust to the changes.

Practising Self-Care for Parental Resilience

Handling challenges and conflicts can be emotionally taxing for parents. Practising self-care is essential for maintaining parental resilience.

Prioritizing Emotional Well-Being

Authoritative parents prioritize their emotional well-being, seeking support and coping mechanisms to manage stress.

Taking Breaks When Needed

Taking breaks and time for self-reflection helps parents recharge and approach challenges with a clear mind.

Seeking Support Networks

Authoritative parents seek support from family, friends, or parenting communities, fostering a sense of community and understanding.

Modelling Self-Care for Children

Modelling self-care for children teaches them the importance of taking care of their own well-being.

Forgiveness and Healing in Parenting

Forgiveness and healing play a significant role in handling challenges and conflicts within the context of authoritative parenting.

Practising Forgiveness

Authoritative parents practice forgiveness, understanding that mistakes and conflicts are a natural part of the parenting journey.

Repairing Relationships

Repairing relationships after conflicts strengthens the parent-child bond and promotes a sense of security and trust.

Embracing the Journey of Growth

Handling challenges and conflicts is an ongoing journey of growth and learning, embracing the imperfections of parenting.

Celebrating Resilience and Progress

Authoritative parents celebrate their resilience and progress in handling challenges, acknowledging their efforts and growth as parents.

As we navigate through the challenges and conflicts of parenting, let us remember that they are opportunities for growth, understanding, and strengthening the parent-child relationship. With love, empathy, and effective communication, we can face these challenges with resilience and create a nurturing and supportive environment for our children to flourish. Let us embrace the transformative power of handling challenges and conflicts in authoritative parenting and continue to grow together as a family.

Chapter 7
Balancing Work and Family Life

HOME
WORK

In the modern world, balancing the demands of work and family life can be a complex and challenging endeavour. In this chapter, we explore the delicate art of achieving a harmonious balance between work commitments and nurturing a strong family bond within the framework of authoritative parenting. We delve into practical strategies, time management, and mindful approaches that empower parents to create a supportive and fulfilling environment for both their professional and parental roles.

The Struggle of Work-Life Balance

Balancing work and family life has become an increasing concern for many parents. The pressures of work commitments, career advancement, and financial stability often collide with the desire to be present and engaged parents.

Understanding the Impact on Family Life

The demands of work can affect family life, leading to stress, limited time together, and potential challenges in parenting.

Prioritizing Family Values

In authoritative parenting, family values take center stage, guiding parents in making decisions that prioritize the well-being and needs of the family.

Fostering a Supportive Work Environment

A supportive work environment that recognizes the importance of work-life balance can significantly impact a parent's ability to manage both roles effectively.

Embracing Flexibility

Flexibility in work arrangements allows parents to adjust their schedules to accommodate family commitments.

Mindful Time Management

Mindful time management is essential in achieving work-life balance. It involves making conscious choices about how time is spent and being fully present in each role.

Setting Clear Boundaries

Authoritative parents set clear boundaries between work and family time, avoiding distractions that interfere with quality interactions with their children.

Designating Family Time

Designating dedicated family time allows parents to engage in meaningful activities and strengthen family bonds.

Establishing Work Routines

Creating structured work routines helps parents stay focused during work hours and efficiently complete tasks.

Balancing Personal Time

Balancing personal time for self-care and relaxation is crucial for maintaining emotional well-being.

Quality Over Quantity

In authoritative parenting, quality time spent with children is prioritized over sheer quantity.

Engaging in Meaningful Activities

Authoritative parents engage in meaningful activities with their children, fostering a sense of connection and joy.

Creating Lasting Memories

Building lasting memories through shared experiences strengthens the parent-child relationship.

Being Fully Present

Being fully present during family time involves active listening and genuine

engagement with children.

Making the Most of Everyday Moments

Simple, everyday moments become opportunities for bonding and connection in authoritative parenting.

Nurturing the Parent-Child Bond

Balancing work and family life requires nurturing the parent-child bond to create a secure and loving environment.

Expressing Love and Affection

Authoritative parents openly express love and affection, reinforcing their unconditional support for their children.

Being Attentive to Children's Needs

Being attentive to children's emotional and physical needs helps build a strong parent-child connection.

Supporting Children's Interests

Supporting and actively participating in children's interests fosters a sense of closeness and shared experiences.

Practising Active Communication

Regular and open communication strengthens the parent-child bond, ensuring children feel heard and understood.

Navigating Parenthood and Career Advancement

In authoritative parenting, parents strive to balance the pursuit of career advancement while maintaining a meaningful family life.

Setting Realistic Career Goals

Setting realistic career goals allows parents to pursue advancement without

compromising family well-being.

Seeking Employer Support

Employer support, such as flexible work arrangements and family-friendly policies, eases the challenges of juggling parenthood and career growth.

Emphasizing Work Efficiency

Efficiency in work tasks allows parents to manage work responsibilities effectively, freeing up more time for family.

Aligning Career Choices with Family Values

Authoritative parents align their career choices with family values, ensuring that their professional pursuits are in harmony with their parenting priorities.

Embracing Parenthood as a Team

Balancing work and family life requires a team effort from both parents, fostering mutual support and understanding.

Sharing Parenting Responsibilities

Authoritative parents share parenting responsibilities, allowing each parent to contribute to the family's well-being.

Communicating Openly about Priorities

Open communication about priorities and responsibilities helps parents align their efforts in balancing work and family life.

Offering Emotional Support

Providing emotional support to one another during challenging times strengthens the parental partnership.

Celebrating Each Other's Achievements

Celebrating each other's achievements in both parenting and careers reinforces

mutual appreciation and encouragement.

Emphasizing Self-Care for Working Parents

Self-care is vital for working parents to maintain physical and emotional well-being amidst the demands of work and family life.

Prioritizing Health and Wellness

Authoritative parents prioritize their health and well-being, recognizing that they need to be in their best state to fulfil their roles effectively.

Finding Time for Hobbies and Interests

Engaging in hobbies and interests outside of work and parenting provides a much-needed sense of fulfilment and relaxation.

Seeking Support Networks

Working parents benefit from support networks, such as friends, family, or parenting groups, who can provide encouragement and understanding.

Creating Restful Spaces

Designating restful spaces within the home allows working parents to unwind and recharge after a busy day.

Managing Parental Guilt

Parental guilt is a common emotion for working parents. In authoritative parenting, managing parental guilt involves self-compassion and realistic expectations.

Embracing Imperfections

Authoritative parents embrace their imperfections and recognize that no parent is perfect.

Focusing on Quality Time

Prioritizing quality time with children over perfection in every aspect of parenting eases parental guilt.

Accepting External Support

Accepting support from family, friends, or childcare services is a part of balancing work and family life, and it does not diminish a parent's love or commitment.

Celebrating Achievements in Both Roles

Celebrating achievements in both parenting and career roles reinforces a sense of accomplishment and self-worth.

Coping with Career Transitions and Family Changes

Career transitions and family changes require adaptable strategies to maintain work-life balance in authoritative parenting.

Communicating During Changes

Effective communication during transitions allows parents and children to navigate the changes together.

Emphasizing Flexibility

Flexibility in adapting to career changes and family dynamics promotes resilience and harmony.

Seeking Support during Transitions

Seeking support from family, friends, or professional resources during transitions helps parents manage stress and uncertainty.

Embracing the Growth Process

Authoritative parents embrace the growth process during transitions, acknowledging that adjustments take time and effort.

Creating Meaningful Family Rituals

Family rituals provide stability and a sense of togetherness, contributing to work-life balance in authoritative parenting.

Establishing Daily Rituals

Daily rituals, such as shared meals or bedtime routines, create opportunities for bonding and communication.

Celebrating Milestones and Achievements

Celebrating milestones and achievements reinforces family bonds and fosters a positive family atmosphere.

Planning Family Vacations and Getaways

Family vacations and getaways offer opportunities to create lasting memories and recharge as a family unit.

Practising Gratitude

Practising gratitude as a family nurtures a sense of appreciation for one another and the blessings in their lives.

As we strive for work-life balance in authoritative parenting, let us remember that it is a journey of continuous growth and adaptation. By prioritizing family values, practising mindful time management, and nurturing the parent-child bond, we can create a fulfilling and supportive environment for both our professional pursuits and our roles as parents. Together, let us embrace the art of balancing work and family life, fostering a loving and resilient family unit where our children can thrive and reach their full potential.

Chapter 8
Nurturing Resilience and Emotional Intelligence

Resilience and emotional intelligence are powerful traits that equip children with the tools to navigate life's challenges, build meaningful relationships, and thrive in the face of adversity. In this chapter, we explore the integral role of authoritative parenting in nurturing resilience and emotional intelligence in children. We delve into the principles, strategies, and practices that empower parents to foster these essential attributes, laying the foundation for their children's emotional well-being and future success.

Understanding Resilience and Emotional Intelligence

Resilience is the ability to bounce back from setbacks and adapt positively to difficult circumstances. Emotional intelligence, on the other hand, is the capacity to recognize, understand, and manage emotions effectively in oneself and others.

The Connection Between Resilience and Emotional Intelligence

Resilience and emotional intelligence are closely interconnected, as emotional intelligence supports the development of coping skills and positive adaptation.

The Benefits of Resilience and Emotional Intelligence

Children with strong resilience and emotional intelligence are better equipped to handle stress, build strong relationships, and succeed in academic and personal pursuits.

Fostering a Growth Mindset

In authoritative parenting, fostering a growth mindset encourages children to embrace challenges and view setbacks as opportunities for learning and growth.

Nurturing a Safe and Supportive Environment

A safe and supportive environment is essential for children to feel comfortable exploring their emotions and developing emotional intelligence.

Building Emotional Awareness

Building emotional awareness is the first step in nurturing emotional intelligence in children.

Encouraging Emotional Expression

Authoritative parents encourage children to express their emotions openly and without judgment.

Identifying and Labelling Emotions

Helping children identify and label their emotions allows them to gain a better understanding of their feelings.

Valuing Emotional Expression

Valuing emotional expression shows children that their feelings are important and worthy of acknowledgment.

Practising Empathetic Listening

Practising empathetic listening when children share their emotions fosters a sense of emotional safety and understanding.

Teaching Emotional Regulation

Emotional regulation is a crucial aspect of emotional intelligence, allowing children to manage their emotions effectively.

Modelling Emotion Regulation

Authoritative parents model healthy emotion regulation by expressing their feelings constructively.

Teaching Coping Strategies

Teaching coping strategies, such as deep breathing or mindfulness techniques, empowers children to handle challenging emotions.

Recognizing Triggers

Helping children recognize emotional triggers enables them to respond more calmly and thoughtfully in difficult situations.

Offering Support During Emotional Difficulties

Offering support and validation during times of emotional difficulty reinforces the importance of emotional well-being.

Cultivating Empathy and Compassion

Empathy and compassion are at the core of emotional intelligence, fostering positive relationships and a sense of community.

Modelling Empathy

Authoritative parents model empathy by showing understanding and concern for others' feelings.

Encouraging Perspective-Taking

Encouraging perspective-taking helps children see situations from others' points of view, enhancing their empathy.

Practising Acts of Kindness

Practising acts of kindness as a family reinforces the value of compassion and generosity.

Engaging in Community Service

Engaging in community service activities provides opportunities for children to extend their empathy beyond the family unit.

Developing Problem-Solving Skills

Problem-solving skills are vital in building resilience, enabling children to face challenges with confidence.

Encouraging Critical Thinking

Encouraging critical thinking helps children analyse problems and consider various solutions.

Fostering a "Can-Do" Attitude

Fostering a "can-do" attitude empowers children to approach problems with a positive and proactive mindset.

Guiding the Problem-Solving Process

Authoritative parents guide children through the problem-solving process, providing support and guidance as needed.

Celebrating Resilience and Effort

Celebrating children's resilience and effort in problem-solving reinforces their confidence and determination.

Promoting Adaptability and Flexibility

Adaptability and flexibility are essential in building resilience, as they allow children to adjust to changing circumstances.

Embracing Change as a Part of Life

Authoritative parents embrace change as a natural part of life, modelling adaptability for their children.

Encouraging Positive Responses to Change

Encouraging positive responses to change helps children approach new situations with an open mind and optimism.

Supporting Transitions

Providing emotional support during transitions helps children navigate through changes with confidence.

Encouraging Risk-Taking

Encouraging calculated risk-taking allows children to step out of their comfort zones and build resilience.

Nurturing Positive Self-Image

A positive self-image is integral to emotional intelligence and resilience, as it cultivates self-confidence and self-worth.

Recognizing and Celebrating Strengths

Recognizing and celebrating children's strengths and achievements fosters a positive self-perception.

Encouraging a Growth Mindset

Encouraging a growth mindset empowers children to view challenges as opportunities for learning and improvement.

Emphasizing Effort over Outcomes

Emphasizing effort and perseverance over outcomes helps children develop a sense of internal validation.

Providing Unconditional Love and Support

Providing unconditional love and support reassures children of their inherent worth and value.

Fostering Coping Skills in Adversity

Coping skills are essential in building resilience and navigating through challenging circumstances.

Teaching Healthy Coping Mechanisms

Teaching healthy coping mechanisms, such as problem-solving or seeking support, empowers children to handle stress constructively.

Encouraging Resilient Thinking

Encouraging resilient thinking involves re-framing negative thoughts into more positive and empowering perspectives.

Emphasizing the Importance of Perseverance

Emphasizing the importance of perseverance and resilience during difficult times builds inner strength.

Providing Emotional Support

Providing emotional support during adversity assures children that they are not alone in their struggles.

Navigating Emotional Challenges

Emotional challenges are a part of growing up, and authoritative parenting helps children navigate through them with confidence.

Validating Emotions

Validating children's emotions during emotional challenges shows understanding and acceptance.

Offering Comfort and Reassurance

Offering comfort and reassurance during emotional difficulties provides a sense of security and safety.

Encouraging Open Communication

Encouraging open communication allows children to share their feelings and concerns without fear of judgment.

Seeking Professional Support if Needed

Seeking professional support, such as counselling, when dealing with complex emotional challenges, ensures children receive the help they need.

Promoting a Growth Mindset in Failure

In authoritative parenting, failure is viewed as an opportunity for growth and learning, rather than a reflection of inadequacy.

Emphasizing the Learning Process

Emphasizing the learning process over achieving perfection encourages children to embrace mistakes as part of their journey.

Encouraging Resilience in the Face of Failure

Encouraging resilience in the face of failure instils a sense of courage and determination in children.

Teaching the Value of Persistence

Teaching the value of persistence and effort in the face of challenges reinforces a growth mindset.

Celebrating Effort and Progress

Celebrating children's effort and progress, regardless of the outcome, fosters a positive attitude toward failure.

As we nurture resilience and emotional intelligence in our children through authoritative parenting, let us remember that these attributes lay the foundation for their future well-being and success. By promoting emotional awareness, empathy, problem-solving skills, and a positive self-image, we empower our children to navigate through life with confidence and resilience. Together, let us foster a nurturing and supportive environment that equips our children with the tools to thrive emotionally and face life's challenges with grace and determination.

Chapter 9
The Role of Self-Care in Parenting

Parenting is a deeply rewarding journey, but it can also be physically and emotionally demanding. In the context of authoritative parenting, prioritizing self-care is essential to maintaining parental well-being, fostering a positive parent-child relationship, and promoting effective parenting practices. In this chapter, we explore the integral role of self-care in parenting, its benefits, and practical strategies that empower parents to nurture themselves while fulfilling their parenting responsibilities.

Understanding Self-Care in Parenting

Self-care in parenting refers to the intentional practice of taking care of one's physical, emotional, and mental well-being. It involves acknowledging and addressing one's needs and ensuring a healthy balance between care-giving responsibilities and personal rejuvenation.

Breaking the Parental Sacrifice Myth

Authoritative parenting challenges the notion of endless parental sacrifice, emphasizing that caring for oneself is not selfish but necessary for effective parenting.

The Link between Parental Well-Being and Child Well-Being

Studies show that parental well-being has a direct impact on child well-being, highlighting the importance of self-care in fostering a positive family environment.

The Role Model Effect

Practising self-care as a parent models healthy behaviours and coping mechanisms for children, encouraging them to prioritize their well-being as they grow.

Embracing the Multidimensionality of Self-Care

Self-care encompasses various aspects, such as physical, emotional, social, and spiritual well-being, each playing a crucial role in overall parental health.

Prioritizing Physical Well-Being

Physical well-being is the foundation of effective parenting, as it impacts energy levels, patience, and overall health.

Ensuring Adequate Rest and Sleep

Authoritative parents prioritize getting enough rest and quality sleep to maintain physical and emotional resilience.

Incorporating Regular Exercise

Regular exercise improves physical health, reduces stress, and enhances mood, benefiting both parents and children.

Nourishing the Body with Balanced Nutrition

Balanced nutrition supports overall health and vitality, enabling parents to meet the demands of parenting with energy and focus.

Seeking Regular Medical Check-ups

Routine medical check-ups and self-care screenings help parents stay proactive about their health and well-being.

Cultivating Emotional Resilience

Emotional resilience is crucial in parenting, as it helps parents navigate through challenges and respond to children's emotional needs effectively.

Practising Emotional Self-Awareness

Authoritative parents practice emotional self-awareness, recognizing and addressing their emotions in healthy ways.

Embracing Emotional Expression

Embracing emotional expression allows parents to process their feelings and prevent emotional burnout.

Seeking Emotional Support

Seeking emotional support from loved ones or professionals provides a healthy outlet for stress and emotions.

Engaging in Mindfulness and Meditation

Mindfulness and meditation practices enhance emotional resilience and aid in managing parenting stress.

Nurturing Social Connections

Social connections are vital for parental well-being, providing support, and reducing feelings of isolation.

Maintaining Supportive Friendships

Authoritative parents maintain supportive friendships that offer understanding and encouragement.

Seeking Parenting Communities

Joining parenting communities and support groups provides a sense of camaraderie and shared experiences.

Investing in Couple Time

Prioritizing couple time and maintaining a strong partnership strengthens the parental support system.

Fostering Family Bonding

Engaging in regular family activities and bonding experiences fosters a sense of connectedness and well-being.

Nourishing Personal Interests and Hobbies

Nurturing personal interests and hobbies outside of parenting enriches parental identity and brings joy and fulfilment.

Carving Out "Me Time"

Authoritative parents carve out time for themselves to engage in hobbies, passions, or hobbies.

Pursuing Lifelong Learning

Continuing to learn and grow in personal interests and pursuits enhances parental self-esteem and self-expression.

Balancing Parenting and Career Ambitions

Balancing parenting with career ambitions allows parents to achieve fulfilment in both areas of life.

Rediscovering Self-Identity Beyond Parenting

Reconnecting with self-identity beyond parenting helps parents maintain a sense of individuality and purpose.

Setting Boundaries and Saying "No"

In authoritative parenting, setting boundaries and saying "no" are crucial aspects of self-care.

Prioritizing and Allocating Time Wisely

Prioritizing tasks and responsibilities allows parents to allocate time efficiently and prevent overwhelm.

Learning to Say "No" When Necessary

Learning to say "no" to additional commitments or obligations helps parents avoid overextending themselves.

Seeking Support in Parenting Duties

Asking for help and seeking support from partners or other family members lightens the parenting load.

Managing Parental Guilt

Managing parental guilt associated with setting boundaries reinforces the understanding that self-care is a necessary and healthy practice.

Embracing Alone Time and Solitude

Alone time and solitude are valuable aspects of self-care that allow parents to recharge and reflect.

Finding Solace in Quiet Moments

Finding solace in quiet moments helps parents rejuvenate and reconnect with themselves.

Creating Restful Spaces

Designating restful spaces at home provides parents with opportunities for relaxation and rejuvenation.

Engaging in Mindful Activities

Mindful activities, such as journaling or meditation, foster self-awareness and inner peace.

Embracing the Gift of Alone Time

Embracing alone time as a gift rather than a burden enhances parental well-being and self-appreciation.

Seeking Professional Support When Needed

In authoritative parenting, seeking professional support, such as counselling or therapy, is an act of self-compassion and strength.

Addressing Parental Stress and Burnout

Addressing parental stress and burnout through professional support ensures the well-being of both parents and children.

Exploring Parenting Challenges

Exploring parenting challenges with a professional helps parents gain valuable insights and coping strategies.

Managing Mental Health and Emotional Needs

Managing mental health and emotional needs promotes effective parenting practices and emotional well-being.

Fostering Personal Growth

Professional support contributes to personal growth and enhances parenting skills.

As we embrace self-care in authoritative parenting, let us recognize that nurturing ourselves is not selfish but an essential aspect of effective parenting. By prioritizing physical well-being, cultivating emotional resilience, nurturing social connections, and fostering personal interests, we strengthen our ability to meet the demands of parenting with love, patience, and joy. Together, let us embrace the transformative power of self-care and create a nurturing and loving environment for ourselves and our children to flourish.

Conclusion

In this journey through the world of parenting, we have explored the transformative power of authoritative parenting - a balanced approach that harmonizes love, discipline, and empowerment. Throughout the chapters of this book, we have delved into the principles, strategies, and practices that empower parents to raise confident, resilient, and empathetic children.

Authoritative parenting is not a one-size-fits-all approach; rather, it is a mindful and adaptable philosophy that evolves with the needs of both parents and children. It emphasizes the value of open communication, mutual respect, and positive reinforcement while instilling important life skills and moral values in the growing minds of our children.

As we conclude this journey, let us reflect on the core principles of authoritative parenting:

Love and Affection: Authoritative parents nurture a loving and secure environment, where children feel cherished and valued unconditionally.

Discipline and Responsibility: Discipline in authoritative parenting is not about punishment but about teaching responsibility and accountability.

Empowerment and Independence: Authoritative parents encourage their children to explore and learn, fostering confidence and independence.

Effective Communication: Open and respectful communication is the key to building strong parent-child bonds and understanding one another.

Resilience and Emotional Intelligence: Nurturing resilience and emotional intelligence equips children with invaluable tools to navigate life's challenges.

Self-Care: Taking care of ourselves as parents is not only crucial for our well-being but also sets a positive example for our children.

In this conclusion, I invite you, dear readers, to reflect on the wisdom and insights gained from this book and apply them in your parenting journey. Parenting is a continuous learning process, and every day presents us with new opportunities to grow alongside our children.

I urge you to share the knowledge gained from this book with other parents, friends, and family members. By spreading the principles of authoritative

parenting, we can collectively create a more compassionate and understanding world for our children to thrive in.

Your feedback and reviews on this book are invaluable to me as an author. I encourage you to share your thoughts and experiences with other readers, as your insights may inspire and support fellow parents in their parenting journeys.

In closing, I extend my heartfelt gratitude to you, dear readers, for embarking on this journey of parenting styles with me. May the principles of authoritative parenting continue to guide you in creating a nurturing, loving, and empowering environment for your children to blossom into compassionate, responsible, and resilient individuals.

Wishing you a fulfilling and joyous parenting experience!

With love and gratitude,

Simi Subhramanian